THE SQUIRREL'S BANK ACCOUNT

**AND
OTHER
CHILDREN'S
SERMONS**

THE SQUIRREL'S BANK ACCOUNT
AND OTHER CHILDREN'S SERMONS

S. LAWRENCE JOHNSON

ABINGDON PRESS, Nashville and New York

THE SQUIRREL'S BANK ACCOUNT AND OTHER CHILDREN'S SERMONS

Copyright © 1972 by Abingdon Press

All rights in this book are reserved.
No part of the book may be reproduced in any
manner whatsoever without written permission of
the publishers except brief quotations embodied
in critical articles or reviews. For information
address Abingdon Press, Nashville, Tennessee.

ISBN 0-687-39268-3

Library of Congress Card Number: 79-186827

To
Our Grandchildren
R. Andrew Foulks, C. Juliette Johnson
and S. Theodore Johnson

PREFACE

One of the most pleasing reviews of my first book of children's sermons, "The Pig's Brother," was published in a South African magazine named "Dimension." The editor wrote: "All too often we judge children's books, or clothes, or furniture, by the impression they make on us as adults—then wonder what is wrong with the children of today who don't appreciate what we do. And so we asked an eight-year-old to read this book."

The eight- to twelve-year-old has been kept in mind in writing these sermons, and they have been tried out particularly on this age group. It is never wise to talk down to children. In fact, one should often use words and language a little above the level of the children. Youngsters who are exposed to a regular series of such sermons will often make it a practice to remember unknown words and look them up in a dictionary.

A children's sermon should be for instruction and not for entertainment alone. It should never be considered as just a pretty story, but as a help to youngsters in their daily lives and their relation to the Bible, morals, ethics, and their church.

Only the unusual child will listen attentively to a sermon developed especially for an adult congregation, but most children will appreciate one delivered just for them. Children, like adults, enjoy preferential treatment.

Hopefully, many serendipities may result from the use of this series.

Much thanks is due my wife, Alice, for her help in the preparation of this book.

S. Lawrence Johnson

CONTENTS

ALL OF A SUDDEN	11
BISCUIT AT THE BEACH	13
WEAVING	16
SYMBOLS	18
IMPRESSIONS	20
WHY?	22
THE CACTUS AND ITS SPINES	25
A BROKEN BALLOON	28
LIVING ALONE	30
BRIGHTY	32
IT'S SO DIFFERENT	34
THE POISON TREE	37
CAN AN ETHIOPIAN CHANGE HIS SKIN?	39
THE FELLOW WHO SLEPT IN CHURCH	42
GOOD ADVERTISING	45
PILLARS	47
WINGS OF A DOVE	49
SAND IN YOUR SHOES	52

FROST ON THE WINDOWPANE	54
THE MILLS OF GOD	56
LIFELINES	58
JUST CHASING	61
BE PREPARED	64
A GOOD FOUNDATION	66
ONE HUNDRED AND SEVEN	68
THE MYSTERY HOUSE	70
CHANGING SANDS	73
HOW DO YOU LOOK?	76
CROSSWINDS	78
PASSING THE CALF	81
RAUWOLFIA SERPENTINA	84
JOSHUA FIT THE BATTLE OF JERICHO	87
THE TREE IN THE LANE	90
THE BURNING BUSH	93
DECORATIONS	95
LOST ISLANDS	97
THE NAME	100
BANQUETING ON A BOOK	102
IT TAKES A LONG, LONG TIME	104
WHAT ARE YOU LOOKING AT?	107
THE HARVEST SEASON	109
THOSE LITTLE THINGS	111
BOXED IN	113
CROSSING THE JORDAN	115
THE MARKS OF CHRIST	118
SUBWAYS	120
THE UNDERTOW	122
THE SQUIRREL'S BANK ACCOUNT	125

ALL OF A SUDDEN

The dictionary is a wonderful instrument. There are so many words we don't understand and whose meaning we cannot guess. In sociology, mathematics, chemistry, and medicine, where new things are being learned, every day new words are being invented. So, we shouldn't be upset if we don't know every word we read or hear. We can all use a good, modern, up-to-date dictionary.

Singing groups have chosen many names. One such group calls itself "The Serendipity Singers." That's a nice-sounding title. It rolls off the end of your tongue like warm syrup. Have you any idea what the word "serendipity" means?

The word was coined by Horace Walpole in 1745 in the fairy tale "The Three Princes of Serendip." Serendip was the former name for Ceylon.

The heroes of this tale were always making happy discoveries by accident. The word thus means the faculty for making happy, unexpected, accidental discoveries.

There are serendipities in all of life if you are alert. Some of the greatest discoveries in medicine have come in just this way. You can find happiness, you can find new and wonderful friends, if you are alert. If you go out of your way to be kind, utterly unexpectedly someone will be kind to you. If you defend some boy or girl, someday you may unexpectedly find someone protecting you. If you refuse to cheat, unexpectedly you may find a boy or girl who admires and respects you and who, because of you, will not cheat.

Jesus said, "Seek ye first the kingdom of God." There are many serendipities which add up to the kingdom of God. The kingdom of God is not something you can precisely define, but it is something you can feel and enjoy. From it you will receive great inspiration.

BISCUIT AT THE BEACH

Biscuit is a little white poodle almost as sweet and loving as your little dog. She had her first experience at the beach when visiting Panama City, Florida, when she was six months old. She quivered when her mistress got out the leashes for her and her mother, Muffin, seeming to recognize an adventure in the offing. As soon as the door was opened, she gave a delighted bark and dashed down the porch steps.

After the group—the master, the mistress, Muffin, and Biscuit—had crossed the road which runs just north of the dunes, the mistress removed the leashes. Biscuit ran into the sparse vegetation growing along the ridge. She hadn't gone five feet before she turned and hurried back, then lay with her feet in the air and began yelping. She was covered with sandspurs, little round balls of prickers which were sharp. Biscuit learned her first lesson of the day: a little dog, just like a little boy or girl, must follow an established path or else be prepared to take the consequences. When the leash had been removed, her master had said "stay" quite sternly. If she had obeyed, her master would have led her and she would have escaped her torment.

The sand on the beaches in that part of Florida is white, hard, lovely, and clean. Biscuit forgot her trouble with the burrs and raced away. Back and forth she ran—up, down, and around. Every once in a while she would turn back and bark, "For goodness sake hurry up, people." Suddenly she spied a sandpiper just at the edge of the water where the waves were breaking. A half-dozen leaps and, surprise, she was in the ocean. Of course, she had had baths in nice warm tub water, but the Gulf of Mexico was cold that March morning. The taste of soap was bad enough when she had her bath but sea water was salty—"ugh."

Biscuit had learned her second lesson of the day. There is an old saying which describes this lesson: "Look before you leap."

Bouncing right back from her fright, Biscuit once more began to run on the beach. Because she wanted someone to join in her fun, she began pestering her mother. Muffin accepted the antics of her tiny pup graciously for a time, patiently turning aside and giving sharp cries of admonition. Blissfully ignoring the warnings, Biscuit was persistently and completely annoying. All of a sudden the old dog snapped at her obstreperous daughter. In utter disbelief Biscuit whined, seeming to ask, "What was the need of that?" She had learned her third lesson: others have rights that need to be observed just as we want our rights to be heeded.

Jesus said, "Seek and you shall find; knock and it shall be opened unto you." All of life is an adventure. However, there are rules. Biscuit's trouble is that she has a short memory, just like some boys and girls.

WEAVING

The Oriental Institute in Chicago houses some remarkable models constructed to show life in bygone days. One is a loom for weaving, like those used in Egypt. Of particular interest is that it differs little from our modern looms. The principle of a loom has not been altered.

Weaving came into being because men and women found animal skins were not as comfortable as woven materials when used as coverings for their bodies. Woven materials could be shaped to follow contours and were also more beautiful.

Many materials were used in weaving. Sheep's wool was the chief one used for family garments. Camel's hair was fashioned into warm cloaks and sometimes into nets. Goat's hair seemed to make the most durable and strongest tents. Sackcloth (today we call it burlap) came from coarse flax

WEAVING

or hemp or goat's hair. The stem of a shrub called ramie, which is of the nettle family and whose fibers are long and strong, produced a strong but lightweight fabric. Cotton was not used until later, at the time of Alexander the Great.

All through life we are weaving what we call our personalities. Just as the materials used in weaving determine the type and texture of fabric, so the basic substances we weave into our personalities determine the finished products. As silk thread makes a beautiful fabric, so kindness, love, consideration make for a fine, appreciated personality.

We gather up the things we learn in school, the things we are taught in church school, the things that happen to us in our various contacts with other people, and we put them together. We have a lot of freedom as to the way we may use these various fabrics. Jesus gave us the finest pattern for our lives. If we wish, we can become like him.

There are two texts worth remembering: From Ephesians: "That we no longer be children . . . but . . . may grow up in all things, like him who is the head—Christ." And from Second Peter: "Grow in grace, and in the knowledge of our Lord and Savior, Jesus Christ."

Many pictures have been created through weaving. These are called tapestries. Some tapestries are beautiful, but some are ugly. So it is with our lives. It takes time, effort, consideration, and concern to produce a good life. Weave a good fabric.

SYMBOLS

A few years ago the word "beatnik" was in fashion. Then the word "hippie" was invented. Right away these words make us think of certain types of persons.

Soldiers wear uniforms. Immediately we can tell classification or rank by the symbol which is on the soldier's arm or his shoulder: a colonel by the eagle, a sergeant by the number of stripes.

In our hymn books we see a mass of symbols. Some are called words and others notes. Both of these indicate certain types of sounds we can make either with our throats or with musical instruments.

When we meet our friends, our "hello" is a particular grunt symbol we call a spoken greeting. We smile—a symbol of affection or approval. When Mother or Dad smiles we are happy, but when they

SYMBOLS

frown we are very careful, knowing this is a warning sign of possible trouble.

Everything in life is indicated or directed by symbols. The chemist uses symbols to say what he is thinking, so does the mathematician. Space vehicles would not be possible without many symbols.

Sometimes people comment that they do not like symbols in the church. What do symbols in the church mean? The cross tells of sacrifice, new life, and the spirit of Christ with us. The triangle speaks of three different sides of God which we call the Trinity. Of course, the candle is light. Jesus said, "You are the light of the world. . . . Let your light shine."

In most church buildings there are many symbols incorporated into the architecture. The alpha and omega, the first and last letters of the Greek alphabet, mean God was at the beginning and will be at the ending. The circle signifies the whole of life. The three rings are not an advertisement for a particular beverage but represent a very old symbol calling our attention again to the three different ways of looking at God.

IMPRESSIONS

A wise man once said, "If you try to make an impression, you probably will." What he meant was, the impression you do make may be the exact opposite of the one you would like to make.

The Grand Canyon is said by geologists to be one of the best places on earth to study the formation and development of the earth. Here is a great storybook, with the tales written in stone.

You may see the footprints of great animals who lived many years ago. Man has named these animals "dinosaurs." Millions of years ago, dinosaurs walked through some mud. Then, either a great wind or rain storm washed soil down over the tracks. In some manner the soil was subjected to great pressure and turned to stone. By leaving their impression these animals provided us with the means to better understand what they were like.

IMPRESSIONS

It was not only heavy animals which left an imprint. Geologists have found impressions of ferns, sea shells, insects, and other things which lived millions of years ago. There are also indentations left by hailstones which fell long ago. Some of these hailstones were large, but others were no bigger than the head of a common pin.

It doesn't take very much to make an impression. In fact, everything we do or say makes an impression. A kind word spoken, an angry outcry, a smile, a frown—none are completely forgotten.

Have you ever had the experience of meeting a boy or girl for the first time and not liking them and later, when you knew them better, finding they were the nicest people? Something they did or said at that first meeting gave you the wrong impression. On the other hand, sometimes people that we think are wonderful when we first meet them turn out not to be nice at all. The first impression they gave, although a good one, was false and untrue.

The apostle Paul wrote to his friends in the city of Galatia: "I bear in my body the marks of the Lord Jesus." How proud he was of this. He always behaved in such a way that when people met him, they were aware that he was trying to be like Jesus. Isn't it worth trying all the time to be so good and worthwhile that people will look up to you, want to be with you, to do as you do, and be as much like you as they can?

WHY?

In nature everything seems to play a part. Often we are upset by the wind and the rain which come destroying. We read in the papers or hear over radio or TV about a tornado which caused great damage when it hit Kokomo, Indiana, or Pontiac, Michigan, or any of a dozen other places, and we ask, "Why?"

We must never forget that wind and rain are not all bad, just as they are not all good either. Winds which can break up houses, schools, and business blocks also can spread pollen to fertilize trees and flowers, can distribute seeds from all kinds of plants. Perhaps some of you have watched the maple seeds whirling and swirling through the air. Or maybe it has been cottonwood seeds, or dandelion fluff, or milkweed seeds you've seen being carried sometimes for miles in the air. Those who are allergic to pollen don't like the wind when it swirls this material around, but this necessary function of the wind is for good.

Without the wind, our forests would be in real trouble. The wind blows the seeds from the trees, deposits them on the ground, and then gently covers them with a blanket of dirt so the little maturing plants may find a place to take root. On a hot summer day, how good a cooling wind can feel! Then may come a severe electric storm, with lightning striking and tearing down the pine or splitting apart an oak or setting fire to a home. The rain comes. The water rushes down the hill, sometimes flooding valleys and carrying away houses and animals. Yet when this happens, we must not forget that if the rain didn't fall our food supply would be cut off. Everything in life depends on moisture.

In the woods a fallen tree decays and gradually becomes compost that it may give life to other trees and to plants. So you see, the wind and lightning may be both good and bad for us.

In life, things happen which seem both good and bad. We must be careful to judge which is good and which is bad. Many people consider death to be the ultimate in what is bad. They cry, "Why did it happen to so and so?" If we really stop to think, we realize that death must happen to each one of us sooner or later and that death is not really bad but ultimately good.

A little boy or girl touches a red-hot stove and gets burned. We say, "That's bad!" But, is it bad? Isn't the experience, the hurt and the blister, a good warning to us not to touch a hot stove again?

There is a balance if we will open the eyes of our minds to see. Jesus said, "Let him who has ears to hear, hear."

THE CACTUS
AND ITS SPINES

"See America First" is a slogan we often hear. It would be wonderful if each one of us could drive through each state in the union, visiting every large city and small town. Each community is so much like every other, and yet each is so different. Some are in warm parts of our nation while others are in moderate or cold areas. Some are in flat country while others are perched on hillsides.

If you made such a tour, you would notice lots of small differences as you drove along. In Alabama and other states in the humid South you would see air conditioners which take moisture from the air. In the dry states of the southwest the air conditioners put moisture into the air.

In the South there are beautiful trees covered

with an abundance of leaves. In parts of our Southwest trees are sparse and very small. In Alabama almost any kind of pine tree will do well. On the rim of the Grand Canyon the pinyon pine is about the only one that will survive.

In the Southwest you will see many cacti, wonderful plants which have adapted themselves to live where there is little water. They have a thick skin so they can conserve moisture, and most of them are covered with prickly spines which discourage hungry and thirsty animals which might be tempted to eat them.

Throughout nature we see this process of adaptation. Certain insects look like leaves and can be seen only by a person who has good eyes. The "walking stick" is a most amusing fellow. He looks like a twig from a tree. He will stand very still, not moving at all, making it almost impossible to recognize him as something alive. The chameleon changes his skin color so he will blend with the rock or leaf.

The boy or girl who is trying to follow the teachings of Jesus must learn this sort of adaptability. It is not easy to learn. A follower of Christ must never let down his principles, yet he must always be able to adjust to every person and situation.

The apostle Paul once said that we must be in the world but not necessarily part of the world. The boy or girl who is considered "square" or "out" or "not turned on" simply is ignored by others and has little or no influence. But if a young person is part of a

THE CACTUS AND ITS SPINES

group, yet outspoken and honest with regard to his convictions, he will be respected.

Go with the gang as far as you can while still remaining true to what you know is right. Remember the cactus. It adapts to the hot climate, but it also has spines to protect itself. We must all adapt, but we must also protect those things we hold dear.

A BROKEN BALLOON

Here is a balloon. As it is blown up, it gets larger and larger. At last it breaks. Although you expected it to happen, you still were startled as it emitted a loud pop.

Driving across the prairies of South Dakota or the deserts of New Mexico, you see deserted farms. Abandoned farms can make you feel sad. Why were these places abandoned? How many tears were shed when some family had to move away? Undoubtedly people came to these spots with great expectations and hopes. They probably planned to carve a place for themselves, to grow enough things to supply their family with food, and have enough left over to sell.

What happened? Many things could have happened. There could have been lack of water so their crops wouldn't grow. There could have been dust

A BROKEN BALLOON

storms such as swept over the Dakotas in the 1930's, when some farms were literally buried with dirt which had been carried miles in the wind.

The abondoned farmhouses or barns stand as skeletons, stark and naked, reminders of the dreams, hopes, and aspirations of the men and women who had to move away. Those dreams vanished like the bursting of a balloon.

We must all try our best all the time, but we shouldn't be disappointed when things seem to go wrong and all our hopes are blasted. Jesus told his disciples, "It is not for you to know the time or the season."

The apostle Paul said, "When I was a child I thought as a child, but when I became a man I put away childish things." As we grow older, many of us continue to think as children, and when we don't get our own way we sulk and cry and get angry.

There is a story of a Scottish king named Robert Bruce who crawled into a cave to rest. As he lay thinking about the failures he had had in battles, he noticed a spider trying to spin a web. Over and over the spider tried to swing across the mouth of the cave but failed. When the spider finally managed to attach its web to the other side of the cave, Robert Bruce might have thought of the valued phrase: "If at first you don't suceed, try, try again."

There must be many broken balloons, many blasted hopes, many abandoned farms in life, but we must always try, try again.

LIVING ALONE

One time a group of boys went with their leader on a camping trip. This man taught the boys many things, usually by example and not by talking at them.

As they sat around the campfire, the conversation turned to attending church. The boys argued about it for quite a while. Some of them thought church attendance was fun. Certain boys said they attended because their parents made them go.

One lad said nothing during the discussion. Then, he spoke indignantly, "Well I don't intend to go to church. I don't get anything out of it."

The leader of the group didn't say a word. He got up picked up a long stick and walked to the fire. With the stick he pulled away a bright glowing ember then went back to his place. They all watched the burning bit of wood as it first grew gray, then turned black. Without the rest of the fire it simply wouldn't burn. The leader had taught a lesson. He didn't need to speak.

There are many people who think they are self-sufficient who believe they can get along without assistance from anyone else. Years ago there used to be quite a few men and women who thought they were serving God by living in caves all alone. Various names were given to these people: solitaries, monks, hermits, and so on. Those who decided to find a tall tree or a pillar and to live alone at the top were called "pillar saints." But, were they saints?

An ancient legend tells of one such man who resolved to spend the last days of his life seeking an increased sense of God's presence. He decided he could best achieve this by retiring to the spire of a great cathedral. There, he thought, he could find quiet for meditation and prayer, away from disturbing influences.

For a long time the busy life of the city swirled beneath his feet. At last, the man felt he was about to die. He appealed to God to show himself. Finally, he heard a faint voice from the distance. He cried, "Where art thou, O Lord? I can hardly hear you." He had to strain to hear the answering voice, "Here I am, down among my people."

BRIGHTY

In the Statuary Hall in Washington, D.C., there are some wonderful statues of men and women who have given much to their country. Each state has taken great pride in statues erected to favorite sons or daughters. Someday your statue may stand in that place of honor.

One of the attractions in the Visitor's Center in Canyon City on the south rim of the Grand Canyon is a statue, not of a great person, but of a little burro. A book has been written about this tiny animal, "Brighty of the Grand Canyon." A statue to a burro—why, for goodness' sake? That's just the reason: for goodness' sake.

If you are in extremely good health, and weigh less than two hundred pounds, and want to, you can make a trip on a burro or mule down into the

Grand Canyon itself. It is a difficult trip that takes you down as much as 3,200 feet below the rim. The thing you must remember before starting this trip is that it is the opposite from climbing a hill or mountain. After you have gotten down, you must climb back up again. This can be a rugged trip, but if you are adventuresome, it is worthwhile.

The wrangler in charge of the mules knows each one of them as well as—and in some cases better than—he knows members of his own family. If you make the trip, he will study you and assign you to the animal he thinks would be best for you.

Brighty was a little burro that carried people down into the gorge of the Grand Canyon. She was a lovely little animal—not pretty to look at perhaps, but she had a marvelous personality. A burro with a personality? Certainly. Your doggie has a personality, doesn't he? Your kitty has traits which make it different from all other cats, doesn't it? So, this burro had a nature which endeared her to everyone who met her. She was always kind and considerate and didn't complain regardless of how hot it was on the trail. When it was extremely hot and she was thirsty, she didn't fuss but did her work properly. When she was offered an apple or given a lump of sugar, she took it with a nod of thanks.

The lesson she taught was simply this: you don't need to do great things to be remembered. All that is necessary is to do your job and do it well, without complaining.

IT'S SO DIFFERENT

The Sierras are young mountains in the history of our world and stretch up big and bold. They are stark, naked, and cold looking, but very beautiful. For thousands of years these mountains have stood as they appear today, a wonderland of glacier-scarred ridges, mysterious valleys, huge gray peaks with thickets of oak and tall somber pines. The giant pines and superb sequoias rise majestically.

The name given to these mountains comes from Spanish and Latin and means "saw." Truly, this is an excellent name, for they are rough and uneven and resemble the teeth of a saw. For much of the year they are covered with snow. Even during the summer some of them still retain large pockets of snow and ice. It is a never-to-be-forgotten experience to drive from the heat of the foothills of Cali-

IT'S SO DIFFERENT

fornia and see ice and snow in July and August and feel the coolness.

As you begin climbing, the first thing that impresses you is the change you can notice in the trees. First there are the pines: sugar pine, yellow pine, Douglas fir, and the wonderful cedar whose incense fills the air. Then there is a belt of trees that are mostly silver fir and red fir. All of a sudden you see tamarack, mountain pine, and hemlock. As you reach the heights, you find scrub pine and tangled dwarf pines, some only a foot or two in height and not more than an inch in diameter.

If you look sharply, you may see many animals. The bears are quite tame and friendly and there is a great temptation to feed them. But you are warned not to do so, for although they seem friendly, they are still wild animals and unpredictable.

The animal population changes as you climb higher, just as the trees do. Besides sheep, there are red squirrels, some mountain goats, a few mule deer, and grizzly bears. Even though you drive rapidly, you can notice the constant changes in the surroundings and the view.

The astonishing thing is that when you come back down from the heights, everything looks so very different from the way it did on the way up. You see the very same things but they appear different. Why?

When you are a little boy or girl, things look completely different to you from what they will when you reach twenty, thirty, or older. We call this developing maturity. A person of fifty wouldn't think of doing some of the things a fellow of fifteen would do because he is aware of what might happen as a result of such behavior. Each year causes us to look at life with what we term "new perspective." The word "perspective" means getting a true picture of something. You don't know what a house is like unless you see all sides of it and go through every room.

There was an old fellow we read about in the Old Testament who once said, "I have heard of you by the hearing of the ear; but now my eyes see you." What he was saying is that as you grow, you gain more experience in life, and you come to know and appreciate God better.

THE POISON TREE

There are many of them—brothers, sisters, cousins, uncles, and aunts—in the family of the "poison trees." They are generally known as the sumac family. They live all over the world. Some members are found in New Brunswick, Canada, some in southern Ontario, others in Minnesota and North Dakota, and more in Georgia and Alabama. Some very vicious members of the family live in South America.

One of this group of trees which you may already know or may meet sometime is called the "Florida poison tree," or to give it its proper name, the "Mentopium toxiferum." This tree rarely grows to more than thirty or thirty-five feet tall. Sometimes its trunk is ten or fifteen inches in diameter. It is a lovely looking tree, with attractive clusters of flowers and lustrous orange fruit. The stout arching limbs and pendulous branches form a spreading, round-topped crown. The sap of this tree is extremely poisonous to the touch.

There are many stories of people who have become acquainted with the poison tree. One such tale will pretty well sum up all of them. A man went into the jungles of Brazil. This man thought he was superior and knew more than his Indian companions. He saw a lovely tree and started toward it. His guides warned him not to go near, saying there were spirits in the tree who would do him harm. He laughed at these silly native superstitions and lay down beneath the spreading branches to sleep. When he awakened, his whole body was puffed and red. He itched so badly he thought he would go mad. For weeks his Indian guides cared for him and eventually nursed him back to health.

There are several lessons we can learn as we think about the poison trees. One of the clearest is this: Jesus said, "Beware of those who come in sheep's clothing and inwardly are ravening wolves." There are boys and girls and men and women who appear great, but who can lead us into all kinds of bad experiences.

CAN AN ETHIOPIAN CHANGE HIS SKIN?

Not just once, but many times the Mississippi River has overflowed its banks. When it flooded near Vincennes, Indiana, a few years ago, people were shown a wonderful illustration of the strength of habit.

Water almost completely flooded a farmyard. The water tank for the cattle, which was some distance from the barn, was kept full by a windmill. The cows were accustomed to plod from the barn to the tank whenever they were thirsty. Now the entire valley was covered with water. In fact, it rose to within three inches of the top of the tank. Yet the cows still plodded from barn to tank for their drinks. Twice one cow got stuck in the mud while trying to reach the tank. Once it nearly drowned, but it persevered until it finally reached its goal and took a drink. Then it turned around and made its way back through the flooded area to higher, drier ground. You say, "That cow was just plain dumb." But wait a minute. Don't be too hard on that cow. Don't people do just such silly things through force of habit?

Watching his grandfather, a little boy asked, "Why do you turn your shoes over and shake them every time you put them on?"

The grandfather was surprised. "I didn't realize I shook them. I guess it's a habit, a habit I began while I was living in India. Scorpions and centipedes very often crawled into our shoes at night. Every morning we had to be careful to shake out our shoes."

Forming a habit is like making a rope which grows stronger every day as we constantly twist in new fibers. New Englanders have the reputation of never accepting anything new. This is not only a habit of those living in the Northeastern states, but of many people in all states as they grow older. They become more and more satisfied with things as they are. They do not want to change; they will not change. Habit becomes the master. The person who has become a slave to a habit we call a "stick-in-the-mud."

It seems that bad habits grow quicker and stronger than good habits, so that sometimes we have habits we need to break. There are some peo-

CAN AN ETHIOPIAN CHANGE HIS SKIN?

ple who have the habit of taking drugs, some who drink too much, some who smoke too much. What is the best way to break a bad habit? First, you have to want to break it. Then you should ask God to help. A group of folks who call themselves Alcoholics Anonymous advise one another to begin each day by saying, "God help me please to control my habit." Then, if they go through the day without taking a drink, before going to bed they are to thank God for keeping them strong.

You have heard the question lots of times, but it's a safe wager not one of you knew that it was first asked by the prophet Jeremiah: "Can an Ethiopian change his skin?"

THE FELLOW
WHO SLEPT IN CHURCH

Years ago in the churches of old New England when sermons used to run two or three hours, a man was appointed to walk around the congregation carrying a long pole which had a hard ball on one end and a feather on the other. When someone didn't sit quietly he might reach out and give them a crack with the ball end. If they went to sleep he would tickle them with the feather.

Did you ever see anyone go to sleep in church? In the book of Acts there is a story of a fellow who did just that. The name of this young man was Eutychus but it might have been Jack, Jim, Jane, or Mary. The scripture reads: "There sat in the window a certain young man named Eutychus who had fallen into a deep sleep, and as Paul was long in

THE FELLOW WHO SLEPT IN CHURCH

preaching, he sank down with sleep and fell from the third story and was taken up for dead."

Lots of Roberts, Freds, Debras, and Marthas have gone to sleep in church, but not many have fallen from the third floor windows, so their stories have not been written.

It is told that one hot Sunday an old preacher in the deep South, noticing that many in his congregation were asleep, paused in his sermon and called a deacon to pass the offering plate. "But the collection has already been taken," the deacon said. The preacher responded, "Never mind that, take up another. There is no reason why they shouldn't pay for their lodging as well as for their spiritual food."

A church school teacher in Salem, Massachusetts, once asked her class if they could make any recommendations to better the church. One girl said she thought preachers shouldn't talk so long. No doubt Paul had been speaking for a long time before Eutychus went to sleep. Paul was only making a one-day stop in the city. He had much to say that he thought these people needed to hear. But the little Salem girl was right—Paul shouldn't have talked so long. He should have done as Jesus did on occasion, stopped, and said, "Let's take time out for lunch."

Besides being tired, Eutychus probably also went to sleep because of poor ventilation in the room. But enough of excusing him. He was only doing what so many people do today: we close our ears when we don't want to be told what is right and what is wrong.

There are a lot of things wrong in this world of ours that might be corrected, like boys and girls not having sufficient food or clothing or being unable to go to school. Some people close their eyes to these things and sort of sleep because they don't want to see or hear how things really are around them.

If you keep your eyes open, and don't go to sleep when you shouldn't, you'll discover there are all kinds of opportunities for fun and for doing good.

GOOD ADVERTISING

On July 19, 1743, in a paper called the "Weekly Journal," there appeared a half-page ad telling about a musical instrument imported from England. This was the first large ad ever carried by a magazine or newspaper. Advertising, though, is very old.

The city of Pompeii, Italy, was covered with ash from a volcano way back in A.D. 79. The ash preserved the city almost perfectly. Today, almost nineteen hundred years later, you may see in Pompeii circus-like posters speaking of things for sale. These were ancient ads.

The old saying, "It pays to advertise," has been proven. Today businesses spend large amounts of money to appeal to boys and girls and their parents, through advertisements in magazines, newspapers, over radio and TV, through billboards, and sky-writing, and goodness knows what else.

An old prophet mentioned in the Bible believed in the value of advertising. Jeremiah called attention to the things he wanted to teach by placing an ox yoke on his shoulders and carrying it.

You, too, are advertisements. Are you good ads for the teachings of Jesus? How do you feel toward boys and girls who have not had the same opportunities you have had? How do you feel toward boys and girls who have skin color different from yours?

A good advertising man knows he needs a slogan. Without doubt, you can repeat many slogans which ad men have devised to sell soap powder or soft drinks. Do you know a good slogan for a Christian? Jesus said, "Go among all nations advertising the good news of the kingdom of God. Advertise it to the whole world and be witnesses unto the nations." So, a slogan for a Christian might be "the good news."

The apostle Paul was an excellent advertising man who used the cross of Christ as his trademark. He said, "God forbid that I should glory save in the cross."

We need to recognize how Christianity makes people different, how it makes them better, how it makes them a more reliable product. Then we need to go out and tell people the "good news." We need to tell them about our trademark, the cross of Christ.

You have something good to advertise. Get going.

PILLARS

In our Bible we read of King Solomon, who built a marvelous temple in the city of Jerusalem. Standing at the front were two very wonderful pillars which added stateliness and grandeur. These were given the names of Jachin and Boaz. They were richly decorated and were supposed to cause the children of Israel to think of God. The tops, which are called capitals, were elaborately carved with lotus flowers, all kinds of leaves, pomegranates, and many other sorts of fruits.

People called them the pillars of the universe, or the pillars that hold the clouds apart, or the pillars which hold the planets in their orbits and the stars in their constellations.

Probably Jachin meant firmness and Boaz strength. Together they said, "God establishes and in him is strength." The priests and politicians used to teach that the pillars represented law and order, the two conditions which they felt were fundamental pillars of our universe.

Girls want to be beautiful. Boys want to be strong. Both seek physical attributes—physical beauty and physical strength. They believe physical beauty and physical strength are the two pillars which can support them through life. A girl supposes that if she can be beautiful, she can have anything or do anything she wants. A boy thinks that if he can be strong, he can become a hero in some branch of athletics.

As a girl grows older, she loses her beauty of face and figure. As a boy grows older, he can no longer excel in physical matches against younger men. Physical beauty and physical strength are like pillars of sand which eventually crumble.

There are such things as inner beauty and inner strength. A girl may develop a personality which makes everyone love her. A boy can build strength of character which will cause others to trust and accept him. Inner beauty and inner strength are like pillars of granite.

WINGS OF A DOVE

Scholars think that King David may have written several of the psalms. Perhaps he wrote the fifty-fifth. It is a lovely poem in which the author admits that at times he has wished for something he couldn't have.

Do you ever wish for something you can't have? Do you ever want to get away from something or some person?

The psalmist says he would like to get away to some quiet valley or to some mountain hideout, preferably by the side of a cooling stream where he could be alone. He wrote, "Oh that I had the wings of a dove and could fly away and be at rest."

King David was not the only one who ever wished for the wings of a dove. At times every man, woman, boy, or girl has uttered some such prayer. When the gang wouldn't let you play with them, did you wish for the wings of a dove? When your Mother asked you to do the dishes, did you breathe such a wish? When Dad said, "Johnny, clean up the yard before you start playing ball," did you wish for the wings of a dove? When you have done something you know you shouldn't have done, or when you've not done something you know you should have done, have you wished for the wings of a dove?

The teacher in a school noticed that one little boy couldn't keep from looking out the window, evidently envying all the birds which seemed to be so free. She called all the children to the window and pointed out that the birds were not playing but working, looking for food. She explained how the robins and cardinals and sparrows were searching for grubs, for flies, and for seeds.

No one can ever reach the top of a mountain just by wishing. You have to do a lot of hard climbing. If you come up against a hard problem or something you don't understand, you've got to face it with all your ability and energy. If you need help, ask for it—but realize that wishing won't wipe the situation away.

What if you did have the wings of a dove? What good would they be to you since you are not a dove? To use the wings of a dove you need the body of a dove. You wouldn't like that, would you? Would there be value in having the legs of the fast-running gazelle if you had the body of a whale? Running away, or trying to run away, from a serious problem is usually apt to create more problems and solve none.

Stop wishing for the wings of a dove. Get to work.

SAND IN YOUR SHOES

Once there was a man who hiked all the distance from the Golden Gate Bridge in San Francisco to New York City. He said the rain, the burning sun, the deserts, the mountains were all hard, but what almost defeated him was the sand in his shoes.

All through life you will find it is not the big things that get you down but the little things. Most people seem to be able to handle the large problems of life, but the minor injustices hurt them.

John became ill. It was a serious illness, but it didn't get him down. Several weeks after he had recovered he overheard someone say, "I think John is mean." For months afterward he worried over that remark.

Fred barked his shins playing football one day and asked to stay on the bench because the pain was so great. Two weeks later he broke his collarbone during a game but continued to play as if nothing was the matter. Why?

Lots of boys and girls live in homes where there is little money, little food, and poor clothing. They are happy boys and girls. Not having things doesn't seem to bother them much. But let some fighting go on between their parents over some unimportant thing, and these same boys and girls get nervous, fussy, and even sick.

Do you recall the story of Samson, who picked up the gate of the temple, but was defeated by the smiles of a girl? Do you remember that the prophet Elijah stood fearless before the king, but began to whimper when he was all by himself? You can never forget that Goliath was able to fight an entire army, but fell before little David and his small sling.

There is a story about Jesus and his disciples finding they were not wanted in a certain city. The disciples lost their tempers much as we probably would have done. Jesus had spent just as hard a day as they, but instead of becoming angry, he simply pointed to the next village. In the gathering dusk, he walked on, smiling.

From earliest times to the present, many people have recognized that it is the little straw and not the huge burden that breaks the camel's back. There are some, thank goodness, who have enough faith and strength to stand up even to the small, gnawing things of life. They are the ones who find it easy to dump the sand from their shoes.

FROST ON THE WINDOWPANE

From the plural of the Greek word "biblion" comes our word "Bible," meaning a collection or library of books. In the Bible there are probably more words of wisdom than in any other collection of books.

The Gospels—Matthew, Mark, Luke, and John—contain the story of Jesus' life and give many of his teachings. In the seventh chapter of Matthew we read that Jesus said to his disciples: "Judge not, that you are not judged." Often we love to complain about mistakes someone else has made, the things they have done that they shouldn't have done, and the things they should have done that they didn't do, all the time forgetting to look at ourselves in the same light.

What happens to us when we judge others? How

FROST ON THE WINDOWPANE

are we affected? How do we make others feel toward us?

If you stand in front of a window on a very cold day, close enough so your breath can blow on it, you will notice that moisture from your breath will condense on the glass. If you continue to blow, as more and more moisture gathers, frost will form. The first thing you know, you can't see through that section of glass to the outside anymore. This is the sort of thing that happens when we pass judgment on someone. Whether our judgment is correct or false makes no difference. Judging beclouds our vision. We no longer see that person correctly.

That is bad enough, but unfortunately that is not all that happens. Our judgment affects the attitude of other people toward the person we are judging. Then, immediately, other people's attitudes toward us are changed. By judging others, we cause people to judge us and we lower ourselves in the respect and admiration of many people.

You cannot throw mud on someone without getting some on yourself. Point your finger at some other child. Now, look carefully at your hand. Notice that three fingers are pointing toward you.

St. Augustine told of a man who prayed to God about his neighbor, saying, "O God, take away this wicked person." God asked, "Which one?"

THE MILLS OF GOD

On the trail along the rim of the Grand Canyon, if you look carefully, you may see bits of rock on which there are some scaly spots. If you ask one of the Park Rangers about those spots, you will learn that they are really black, yellow, and orange plants called lichens.

Really these lichens are two distinct kinds of plants, one a fungus which is of the same family as mushrooms, the second, alga, a cousin of seaweed. These two forms of life are dependent upon each other. The fungus is hard and gives protection to the alga. The alga, in turn, manufactures the food for both kinds of plants. Alone, either plant would die, but together they live and do a very important job. The lichen growing on the rock produces a kind of acid. This acid dissolves the rock so that, little by little, the rock is turned into soil. This takes a very long time, but God has a long time in which to do things.

You can often observe this kind of thing taking place in nature. The leaves turn red, gold, and purple in the fall and drop to the ground. The wind blows the leaves into piles; the rain comes. The leaves gradually decompose and become humus. That is, they return to the dirt from which they came.

There are lessons here we can learn. There is a balance in nature; left alone, all things work for good. Man can and does upset this balance very often. Either he thinks he knows better than God, or he gets greedy, or both. Sometimes man kills birds because he thinks they eat too much grain. Then the fields are overrun by insects which, under natural conditions, would have been eaten by the birds he destroyed.

A second lesson is that there are many things that cannot be done in a hurry. How often you and I want things done, not today or tomorrow, but yesterday. God takes a long time to do things. He doesn't try to hurry things as you and I do.

Henry Wadsworth Longfellow, in a poem which he named "Retribution," wrote:

> Though the mills of God grind slowly
> Yet they grind exceeding small.

The psalmist, thinking in the same terms, reminds us: "One day is with the Lord as a thousand years, and a thousand years as one day."

LIFELINES

In telling of his adventures exploring the North and South Poles, Admiral Richard E. Byrd recounts one horrifying experience. To do special studies, he had set up a small camp a short distance from his base. In order not to become separated from his shelter when making night observations, he planted a lifeline of bamboo stakes in the snow.

For some unknown reason he went beyond his line of stakes one night. He relates that he had taken about one hundred steps when he had a sinking sensation and found he was lost. Fortunately, he did find the stakes and made his way back to safety.

Exploring caves is real fun. Two young men entered the Stage Barn Caverns in South Dakota several years ago. They went deeper and deeper into the cave, thrilled by the beauty they found. After they returned to the surface, they met friends and went to dinner. In discussing the exploration with these friends, Frank said, "Never before have I been afraid of being lost; but for a time, crawling through a wet section, I really became scared." Terry choked on a mouthful of food before blurting out, "I've never before felt a fear of being lost either, but there was a time during our exploring when I was petrified." Both admitted they had kept their fears to themselves so the other wouldn't become frightened too. Each of them had held up a lifeline of courage for the other.

"Earl Haines is lost!" That was the cry heard in a tiny English village. Six-year-old Earl had last been seen at the edge of a hilly picnic area. The search lasted two days before the little boy was found.

What is the purpose in telling these stories? Big people use the word "salvation." What salvation means is getting found after you have been lost.

People can become lost in many different ways. Jesus taught that people could get lost from God and that each person has a responsibility to try to find his own way back to God. He told of a boy who got lost from his father and also about a woman who lost a coin. We read that the boy "came to himself" and sought his father, and that when the boy reached him his father ordered a fat calf be prepared for supper in honor of the occasion. The woman searched and searched until she found her coin, and all her neighbors were happy with her.

Admiral Byrd, by carefully walking back and forth, and counting his steps, found the line of bamboo stakes. The boys in the cave kept control of their emotions and worked their way out of the cave. Little Earl said, "I just sat still like a good boy when I got lost cause I knew if I stayed in one place someone would find me."

When men, women, boys, or girls become lost from God, they can be found, but they must follow the teaching of Jesus that each has a responsibility to try to find his own way back to God.

JUST CHASING

Once there was a big black dog named Nero who was a very popular dog in his neighborhood. All the children liked him because he was gentle and would play with them. Mothers and Dads liked him. They felt he was a reliable dog.

Nero had a very silly trick. He would chase his tail. Around and around he would go until he practically dropped from exhaustion. Around and around he would go, but he never got anywhere.

There are a lot of people who spend most of their lives just chasing around like Nero. Around and around they go, never getting anywhere. Some folks are so busy making money or building up reputations that they never stop to consider where they are going or the true worth of the things they seek.

THE SQUIRREL'S BANK ACCOUNT

Many younger people are questioning the value of this constant drive for things. To show their rejection of this particular way of life, some of them drop out of school and work very hard at doing nothing. Unfortunately, they don't seem to realize that they, too, are just chasing around and getting nowhere.

John D. Rockefeller, the famous rich man, admitted that in the first few years of his life he was too busy making a fortune to enjoy himself and for the next few years he was too busy trying to keep his money. He spent the last few years trying to find a doctor who could help him enjoy food. This rich man said, "I'd give all I have to enjoy a good meal." What did he gain by chasing after the dollar?

In Germany, Adolf Hitler gave himself for one purpose: to gain power. When he was powerful and ruled Germany, he directed that six million Jews be killed. People lived in great fear of Hitler. What did all his power gain for him? In the end he took his own life. All his chasing after power brought him unhappiness.

A former university professor lost his sight shortly after he retired. He learned how to type after becoming blind and now he writes many letters each day to any of his former students who may have illnesses or are in need of encouragement. It is said this man can remember by name every single young man or woman who was ever in one of his classes, so he will always have someone to whom he can write notes of encouragment. He is a happy old man.

JUST CHASING

Early in life he learned that just chasing after things is not very worthwhile.

If you really want happiness, you'll find a lot more of it if you try to do things for other people instead of just chasing after something for yourself.

BE PREPARED

When knighthood was in flower, families were known not only by their names, but especially by what was called their "coat of arms." There was no way to tell if a knight was friend or foe when he was all dressed in his armor, with his face covered by a helmet. Few people knew how to read, so a written name on his armor would not have helped. A way of identification was devised which was simply names in pictures, or "coats of arms."

The most admired coats of arms were those granted by royalty. There were knights in the Holy Land at the time of the Crusades. The hot sun had almost barbecued the men in their armor, so they attached animal hides to their helmets, letting the skins hang down their backs. The coats of arms of these knights were "mantled," or drawn on a background suggestive of an animal skin.

BE PREPARED

A Scottish family living on the border between Scotland and England had a very pretty coat of arms. Beneath the picture was printed in Latin the motto: "Beware, I am ready." The head of this family had the title Lord of the Marches. This sounds as if he was in charge of the marching to battle, but it refers to the family's duty to guard the border, or "march," of the country. The family motto said they were prepared to guard.

Today trailering is very popular, not only in the United States but all over the world. When you go trailering, you must be prepared. You must carry with you all the things you will need—canned goods, clothing for all kinds of weather, lights, sleeping equipment, and all sorts of things. The same is true for hikes or canoeing trips. You need to be prepared.

Life is like going into a strange country or on a trip. You need to be prepared. You need to do your schoolwork. You need to learn all you can. You must also be prepared with good behavior. You need to learn the difference between right and wrong.

A general once said to the children of Israel, "When you have girded on your weapons, you are ready to go up into the hills." Apparently some men had wanted to move without being prepared.

Many boys and girls belong to the Boy Scouts or the Girl Scouts. Whether or not you are a member of one of these groups, you probably know the Scout motto: "Be Prepared."

A GOOD FOUNDATION

A number of cities in the United States, and in countries all over the world, have been built on the sides of mountains. There are homes on Red and Shades Mountains in Birmingham, Alabama, which seem to be hanging right out in the air. Actually they are, but the secret is that these homes all have solid foundations and are anchored firmly into the mountainside.

Every year hurricanes rip into areas in some states. One hit north of St. Petersburg, Florida, several years ago, doing frightful damage. Trailers which had no foundations were tossed and turned. Beach houses were smashed and broken. Loss in time, money, and energy was great. Although people knew such a storm was possible, they took no precautions. Many of us act this way.

A GOOD FOUNDATION

Young people drive cars at excessive speeds, knowing that others who have been speeding have had serious accidents, perhaps have even been killed. They evidently believe it can't happen to them.

A long time ago Jesus told a story about two men who built houses. One made certain he had a good foundation and built on solid rock. The second man found a site which was pleasing to him and his family and built his home there. The fact that the ground was sand didn't seem to bother him. You know what happened when the storms came.

What kind of foundations do we need for life? We all know, if we stop to think for a moment. We need good health. Most of us are blessed with good bodies. We can keep them in excellent shape by proper exercise and by eating the right foods. But what do a lot of us do? We lie around during spare time watching TV, saying we'll exercise tomorrow. We stuff ourselves on candy and potato chips and refuse to eat vegetables and variety meats.

We need good education. We need to study and work hard, and not try to slip by without applying ourselves.

We need to have a firm foundation in religion, too. We need to know basic moral laws and become skilled in following them. There are some who think they can continue to violate laws. They can do so for a while, but when the storms come, then what?

ONE HUNDRED AND SEVEN

Can you imagine living to be one hundred and seven? It does happen now and again, but probably you have never met a person who was that old.

Miss Mary lived to be one hundred and seven. It's a shame you couldn't have known her. She was a wonderful woman. When she was a hundred and three she used to talk about the things she had done in her girlhood—back when she was about eighty. Strangers hearing Miss Mary talk this way gave her funny looks, no doubt thinking she had taken leave of her senses. But she was serious—to her, back when she was eighty seemed like her girlhood.

Miss Mary taught school until she was seventy-five. Then, because others thought she was too old to teach, she retired. As she spoke of her life, she would say, "After I retired, I loafed until I was eighty. Then I got tired of being an old woman the way people wanted me to be." She went to Switzerland for a visit. What fun she had. She walked everywhere. There doesn't seem to be a corner of Zurich or Geneva which she didn't see. She explored the Jungfrau, the Matterhorn, and took two boat trips around Lake Lucerne. Finally she returned to the United States and went back to school to study Russian. When she decided she had gained a good enough grasp of the language to permit her to visit that country, she went to Russia. Now to visit Russia just before the Revolution was something few Americans would have undertaken. But she did.

When Miss Mary was about one hundred and five her best friend died. It was the responsibility of her minister, a young man still in his twenties, to inform Miss Mary of the loss. He was properly sobered by the task. But this dear old lady destroyed the grave mood as soon as he had delivered his message. With twinkle in her eye, Miss Mary said, "I always told that old woman I'd outlive her."

Miss Mary's last illness was short. She was up on a stepladder, wallpapering one of the rooms in her home. The step on which she was standing broke. The fall was more than her frail body could stand.

This grand old lady had all the hurts and aches, the sorrows and pains, that other people have, but she never let any of those things get her down. She could easily have become an old woman, a grouch, but to the day of her death she remained happy in spirit and a girl at heart.

THE MYSTERY HOUSE

In San Jose, California, is a very strange building called the Winchester Mystery House. This is perhaps one of the most peculiar structures ever built. It contains 160 rooms and sprawls over six acres. It was the home of Mrs. Sarah L. Winchester.

Sarah was a lovely woman who married the son of the man who developed and manufactured the famous Winchester rifle. Suddenly, her husband died. Mrs. Winchester was crushed by his death. She feared that those people who had been killed by Winchester rifles would come back to haunt her. She had always been interested in the occult, so she consulted a seeress who told her that as long as she continued building, she would never die. For thirty-six years Mrs. Winchester kept adding to her house.

THE MYSTERY HOUSE

There was no plan for this house. Rooms were added at will, with one-story sections joined to five-story ones which in turn were joined to three- or four-story ones. Stairs were installed which went nowhere, just up to the ceiling. Some of the inside rooms had screened windows and doors. There were secret passageways. There were doors opening onto blank walls. There were trap doors opening onto solid floors two inches beneath.

Because she was afraid people were talking about her, Mrs. Winchester had rooms constructed so she could spy on her servants, or anyone who might be in the house, without being seen herself. Speaking tubes were located so she could hear conversations. They were very much like our modern "bugging" devices.

Connected to the house is a large warehouse where are stored hundreds of objects—wonderful silver and bronze, beautiful doors, valuable art, stained glass windows, lighting fixtures, and many woods for finishing the interior of her projected building.

Of course, all this building didn't prevent death from finally taking Mrs. Winchester, although she did live to be eighty-five.

Fear and guilt are among the worst enemies we can have. Mrs. Winchester feared that when she died she would meet the souls of all those who had been deprived of life by a Winchester rifle, that they would be waiting to stand in judgment upon her.

THE SQUIRREL'S BANK ACCOUNT

A wise boy or girl tries to live so that fear cannot gain any room in his mind. Jesus said, "Fear not, I am with you. If you have the faith the size of a little grain of mustard seed, you need not have fear."

CHANGING SANDS

There is black sand, brown sand, red sand, yellow sand, white sand, and every range of color between.

You can have no more exciting and exhilarating time than walking along a sand beach. At one spot the sand may be hard packed and walking will be easy. Then, in comes the tide. What happens? The sand has shifted. It is as difficult to walk in it as it is to trudge through snow.

Since early man, people have called attention to footprints in the sand. Men have likened the footprints to life and the great changes which come in each person's life. Walk along the beach sometime and then look back. There are your footprints. It is fun to study them. You thought you were walking along in a straight line, but your prints show you were wandering back and forth. No matter how hard you try, it is almost impossible to walk in a straight line. In fact, the harder you try, the more difficult it becomes and the more you go from side to side.

As you walk along the beach, you are going somewhere. It may be toward a bit of driftwood on the shore, or a clump of grass, or a high hump on the dunes. It might even be toward a discarded can reflecting the rays of the sun. The important thing is that you keep walking until you get to the thing or spot you chose. Even though the going may sometimes be difficult, even though you may have wandered back and forth, you do reach your destination. This is true in all of life. Keep your eye on the goal and keep walking till you get there.

You can leave the beach and then return some hours later. The tide will have come and gone. Your footprints will have been washed away. The sand has once more been shifted. It is the same sand, but it appears to be different. Each grain has been repositioned. It is the same with our lives. We live in a house, we go to school, we go to church. We see people, sometimes the same ones over and over again, but in different ways.

For many hundreds of years man has used changing sand to remind him of his life. Have you seen what is called an hourglass? Sand timers have been made in many sizes. Most common for us today are the three-minute timers, used for boiling an egg or timing a phone call. The sand runs from the top portion of the glass through a narrow waist into the bottom section.

John Greenleaf Whittier in the "Centennial Hymn" wrote:

> Our fathers' God! from out whose hand
> The centuries fall like grains of sand.

HOW DO YOU LOOK?

People who live on the Canadian or Mexican borders have some advantages which the rest of us do not enjoy. If you lived in Detroit and liked jams or pork pies, you would be fortunate because, by simply driving through the tunnel or over the bridge, you might indulge yourself. Those who have been fortunate enough to sample "fish and chips" on an English street corner can have a similar delightful experience eating this delicacy in Windsor, Ontario.

There are a number of places where United States and Mexican cities are separated by only a fence and it is a simple matter to pass from one country to another. In Mexican border towns, there are many attractive goods for sale: handcrafted leathers, fine silver pieces, wooden carvings, baskets, shawls, and piece goods. In the air is a delightful odor coming from pocketbooks, billfolds, and other leather goods, which have been decorated by highly skilled artists. There is also the pleasant aroma of tacos, enchiladas, burritos, and highly seasoned beans and rice.

Of course, towns that are next to each other on a border are strongly influenced by one another and there is a natural flowing of culture. This is not as noticeable between Canada and the United States as it is between Mexico and our country. The reason probably is that we share a mother tongue with the Canadians.

Visiting two such border cities as Mexicali and Calexico is really fun. One of the most thrilling and stimulating parts of the experience is watching people. Clerks in stores and checkers at cash registers are bilingual; that is, they speak both Spanish and English. As you approach them, they need only to glance at you to tell which one of those two languages you use. It is uncanny. They never seem to make a mistake.

Did you ever stop to think that how you act speaks before you open your mouth? There is an old adage, "Actions speak louder than words." Just by looking at a person you can tell a lot about him. Remember, too, that just by looking he can judge you. Are you neat? Is your hair combed? Are your finger nails clean? Do you stand up straight?

What do the answers to these questions tell others about you? Are there other questions you might ask yourself?

CROSSWINDS

A man and his wife were about to take a trip from the East to the West Coast pulling their small house trailer behind their car. They had never driven in the western part of the United States, so before leaving, they asked advice of many people who had already had the experience.

Don Rankin said, "I have but a single suggestion. When you see a sign 'Wind Currents' or 'Strong Winds' or the like, pay strict attention to these warnings."

The couple drove many miles without seeing such a sign. However, driving south from Carlsbad, New Mexico, one day they were startled to see the warning: "Crosswinds." Immediately, they paid attention. It was a beautiful day, the sky was clear, the sun was shining brightly. As they rode along, keeping below fifty miles an hour without feeling any wind, they began to wonder why Don had warned them and what crosswinds were.

Some miles further a second warning sign appeared at the side of the road. Once again they heeded the warning slowed down to under fifty miles an hour. Suddenly, it felt as if a mighty hand had taken hold of their car and trailer and was shaking it, as a dog might shake a towel. The car trembled. The trailer rocked from side to side. The day was still clear and bright. The sun continued to shine beautifully. Had they maintained a sixty-five-mile speed, had they not been ready, they might have lost control of the automobile and been plunged over a cliff, falling hundreds of feet below the roadway.

Often your Mother or Dad says, "Don't do that!" or "Be careful!" You don't pay any attention. Many times nothing happens and you say to yourself, "The old squares had nothing to worry about. They were just talking. I wish my parents wouldn't act so silly." But the next time, or the time after that, if you don't pay attention and you severely hurt yourself, don't cry and fuss and try to blame someone else for your own stupidity.

In the book of Romans in our Bible we read: "The wages of sin is death." These words mean just what we have been thinking about. If you don't do what is right, or if you do something you shouldn't, you are apt to suffer. Or what's worse, you are apt to cause someone else to suffer. It is wise to pay attention to the warning signs saying "Crosswinds" because they may be very cross winds.

PASSING THE CALF

In the book of Exodus there is a story of how Moses, leaving the children of Israel, went to the top of a mountain, alone, to talk with God. It was at that time God gave him what we now call the Ten Commandments.

It seems that Moses was away from camp more than a month—long enough for the people to become concerned about him. Questions asked around the campfires were, "Where is he? What is he doing? Why has he been gone so long?" As long as Moses was with them, they felt that God was there too. But when he went away, they were filled with doubt. They began to remember and talk about the gods they had known and worshiped in Egypt. They recalled the old rituals. A large number of the people began to practice some of the things they had been taught in the temples. This gave them something really exciting to do. In the worship of Yahweh, the God of Moses, there were no wild songs, no frenzied dances, but before the gods of Egypt they could really let themselves go.

You may have heard the saying, "When the cat's away, the mice will play." This was the situation among these children of Israel. They went to Aaron, the older brother of Moses, and asked him to make an image of a calf which they could worship. Aaron got them to gather together all their gold and had the metalsmiths melt it all down and cast a golden image. A celebration was proclaimed.

The celebration was just coming to a climax when Moses returned. The people had been eating and drinking too much and were behaving like silly children. Moses was very angry. He was particularly annoyed with his brother for having allowed the people to get out of hand. He shouted, "What's the idea? Why have you let them behave this way?" Aaron whimpered, "Don't get angry with me, Brother. You know how people are. They said, 'Make us a god to go before us.' What could I do? I told them to bring gold and throw it in the fire and, well, you'll never believe this, but that calf came out of that fire."

You see, when Moses accused his brother of doing something he shouldn't have done, Aaron tried to "pass the calf" or, in our slang, pass the buck.

At once he tried to blame someone else or something else. He didn't have the strength to say, "I'm sorry. I did wrong. I'll try to make amends."

Aaron told a lie. He said, "They threw the gold into the fire and out came this calf." Do you do this sort of thing too?

RAUWOLFIA SERPENTINA

God is showing himself to us all the time in many different ways, but you and I are funny in that we never want anything that comes easily. We never want to recognize anything that is simple. We feel it must be complicated to be good.

There is a very important drug used in medicine. Millions of people take it every day. Over the past several hundred years, millions more could have been using it, but it has only been generally available for a short time. Long ago in Bengal—a region of India—men were aware that when a little mongoose got into a fight with a snake and was bitten, he would rush to eat the leaves and roots of a plant which we now call Rauwolfia serpentina. For a short while the mongoose would seem to be drugged, then he would recover and continue his battle with the snake.

Men began to chew small bits of this plant, perhaps to see what it would do to them. They found it had a very quieting effect, much the same as a tranquilizer prescribed by a physician today. But the value of this drug went relatively unnoticed for hundreds of years.

It was not until 1930 that an Indian scientist (remember we are speaking of a man who lived in the country of India, not an American Indian) began to take note of Rauwolfia serpentina and break it apart to try to see what was in it and what it would actually do to men and animals. Still, the scientific community gave little attention to the discoveries until 1949, when a report was printed in the "British Heart Journal." This article acknowledged that the powdered root of this plant seemed to lower blood pressure.

We know little about what causes high blood pressure, but we do know that many people in our modern world suffer from it. Permitted to continue, high blood pressure can be very harmful. Not many of you boys and girls have high blood pressure yet, but as you grow older, in our rushing, competitive world, you may someday hear your doctor tell you, "I guess we'd better try a little reserpine, or reserpine in combination with some other things, to see if we can lower your blood pressure." Reserpine is the name given to one of the very effective extracts of Rauwolfia serpentina.

God is all about us. Men have known that God has been here since the beginning of time. But man has rarely been willing just to accept God. It seems as if it has always been necessary for man first to deny God, to argue about him, to question and say, "But I can't see God; I can't feel God; I can't smell him. I wonder if there is a God."

All we have to do is to be quiet and invite God to enter into our hearts and souls. Then we can have knowledge of him, feel his comfort. We are told that once God said, "Be still, and know that I am God."

JOSHUA FIT
THE BATTLE OF JERICHO

Although God chose Moses to lead the children of Israel out of Egypt to the Promised Land, he did not permit him to enter it. Moses died on the top of Mount Nebo. Then a fellow named Joshua became leader.

Archaeologists seem to have proved many of the exciting stories that cluster around Joshua. One of these is about the taking of the ancient city of Jericho. The digging and searching of the ruins of this old city began in the 1890's, but the outstanding finds were made by John Garstang of Liverpool University, England, between 1930 and 1936.

The children of Israel camped across the river from Jericho near a village called Shittim. Joshua sent men over to investigate Jericho. The spies stayed in the home of a woman named Rahab. News of their being in the city soon reached the king, who sent soldiers to arrest them. Rahab hid her guests under some straw on the roof. In return for saving them, the spies promised that when the children of Israel took the city, they would spare her home if she hung a scarlet thread from one of her windows.

Jericho had the reputation for being so strong that it could withstand an attack. Joshua made no attempt to go against the city until he knew everything he possibly could about its fortifications and the army which was guarding it. Don't imagine, though, that the taking of the city even then was an easy task. From the spies, Joshua learned that the people of the city were morally weak. He believed that rumor could probably accomplish more destruction than armed attack. So, he used the weapon of rumor to generate fear among his enemies.

It was God who directed Joshua in the method for conquering the city. They were to march around the walls once each day for six days and on the seventh were to march around seven times, with the priests blowing horns. To the frightened children of Israel these directions must have seemed silly. They had heard of the great strength of Jericho. How could they possibly conquer the fortress by marching around the walls and blowing the trumpets?

Now, the people in Jericho had been told the children of Israel were not allowed to do any work or any fighting on the Sabbath, the seventh day of the week. Therefore, when the Israelites began to walk on the seventh day, the people in Jericho were scared silly. We are told that the walls came tumbling down and the people gave up without the children of Israel having to lift a sword. Geologists show that it is possible an earthquake tremor caused the walls to fall. But whatever happened, the impossible task of taking Jericho had been accomplished.

The children of Israel had faith in their God and followed his directions, so the task was accomplished. Never say a job is impossible until you give it a try.

THE TREE
IN THE LANE

Trees and vines have all sorts of shapes. They come in many sizes. Their leaves may be big or little and in a variety of colors. Jesus noticed all of these things. One time, in order to tell his followers how much he loved them and how close they were to him, he said, "I am the true vine and you are the branches."

A man living near Ann Arbor, Michigan, has some large orchards. For the most part, he grows pears, apples and plums. He must spray them at the right times, so that insects don't get a chance to eat either the fresh little leaves or the ripening or ripened fruit. He needs to cultivate, or shake up, the ground. He must give the trees the right foods and prune them properly. He must remove certain branches

THE TREE IN THE LANE

and twigs so that those remaining will not be crowded. Then the light from the sun can penetrate to the inner parts of the tree and to each fruit.

An orchard keeper often changes the character of his trees by grafting. To graft is to take a branch from one tree and cause it to live and grow on another tree. Because of grafting, some trees may bear as many as six or more different kinds of fruits.

Have you a favorite apple? Some boys and girls are particularly fond of the Red Delicious apple. Now, the Red Delicious all started with one tree which a man noticed was different. He began to graft branches from it on to other trees. Today there are thousands of Red Delicious apple trees.

Sometimes, as you ride along the road with your parents, you may notice trees growing outside an orchard, outside the fence. The Michigan gentleman has such a tree growing outside his orchard. He says, "It's just a poor old pear tree." But every time he wants a pear to eat, he goes to this particular "poor" tree.

The Golden Delicious apple came from a tree outside a fence. The man on whose property it was found said that it just grew in the lane. There is definitely a lesson here for us. There are boys and girls who are outside our little circle of friends, who are perhaps fine, whom we would enjoy if we would get to know them. They may not have had the same advantages as we have had. They may not have had the same care as we, but that doesn't necessarily matter. We should never turn away from other boys or girls just because they come from a different part of town or because they may have skin which is a different color from our own.

There are many trees growing in the lane. There are boys and girls who do not go to the same school as we do, who do not belong to the same church as we do, or perhaps do not have such nice clothing as we do.

Once a group of men brought to Jesus a woman they said was bad, and they told Jesus she should be punished. Jesus looked at the men but didn't say a word. He stooped down and with his finger wrote in the sand, "He who is without sin among you, let him throw the first stone." This woman was a tree growing in the lane. She was a human being who deserved consideration and friendship.

Trees in the lane can be cultivated where they are, but they can also be moved into the orchard. The man who developed the Red Delicious apple for us paid thousands of dollars for a tree growing outside an orchard. He had it moved into his orchard. When it received care, the tree profited him more than any of the other trees which he owned.

THE BURNING BUSH

For three years Moses took care of the sheep of a man named Jethro, who later became his father-in-law. Moses was a good shepherd. He knew each of the animals in the flock. He knew which were careful, which could be counted on to get their ears torn by briers, which would whimper when he would cleanse their wounds with wine. He would take the baby lambs into his arms. All the sheep seemed to love him from the time of their birth.

When spring came, he would lead his flock to hills where there were bits of green. One day, seeking better pasturage, he drove his flock around the back of a mountain named Horeb. When the cooling evening breezes came, he sat down to eat his supper. He thought back to his days at the courts of the Pharaoh and all the good times he had known there, of what a different life this was for him. He remembered his mother, Jochebed, and the stories she had told him to keep him conscious of being a Jew.

As the sun began to set across the valley, suddenly he saw a strange sight in the darkening shadows—a bush burning. At first he couldn't believe his eyes. As he drew near, he heard a voice calling him by name. He listened carefully. He knew he was hearing the voice of God.

Throughout history, many people have seen in fire something emblematic of the divine. The Bible relates several experiences where God revealed himself to different men through fire. Really, when we think about it, of all the forces of nature fire is perhaps the best way of picturing God. Fire is not only pure and bright and terrible, but also comforting.

God revealed himself to Moses through fire, not only to arouse his curiosity, but to teach lessons. God does not need to make a display of himself. Had he wanted, he might have lighted up the entire mountain. Instead, he appeared in a small flame. Moses was intelligent enough to know this.

God also showed Moses that God was not material but could be in the material. To us, this doesn't sound important, for we already know it to be a fact, but in Moses' day men worshiped gods of stone, wood, and metal.

Moses also was taught to recognize that his God was gentle. Not one twig of the bush was hurt. God does not destroy. God creates.

DECORATIONS

There are many ways to learn about life as it was lived in ancient communities, but there is none better than studying the manner in which people decorated their homes and public places. These decorations are like picture books of the past.

Archaeologists, those men and women who dig where cities once stood and carefully study their findings, can tell volumes about the people who once lived in a particular place by the glaze, marks, or decorations on the pottery pieces they fit together.

In A.D. 79, Vesuvius, a volcano in western Italy, blew up, scattering thousands of tons of dirt and ashes over the countryside. The ancient city of Pompeii was buried, in some places beneath sixty-five feet of dirt. Men constructing an aqueduct across the site in 1594 realized where the city had been buried, but it was two hundred years before a concerted effort was made to uncover the ruins. Much of the old town has now been laid bare. If you went there to visit, you would notice how straight and modern looking the streets are. You would enter some of the old homes and public buildings and be fascinated with the pictures which were set in the floors with little bits of stone. You would be intrigued by the paintings on the walls and by the beautiful vases and other pottery. On some of these articles the pictures stand out from the surface in what we call bas-relief.

In caves of southern France you may see decorations on the walls which were painted there by prehistoric men. These pictures were well done, in color. By studying them, we are able to learn how these people lived.

The Egyptians buried their dead in cave-like tombs which were beautifully decorated. There was an ancient Egyptian pharaoh named Tutenkhamon, generally referred to as King Tut. In his burial place were found lots of furniture, pottery, gorgeous pictures, ornamental doors, rugs, and coverings for walls. All these things give us an intimate picture of life at the time when King Tut was alive.

Have you ever stopped to think how much people can tell about you by the way you act, the things you do or say? If you say dirty things, or things that are not right, people will know what you are. They will realize what is in your mind by the dirty decorations.

LOST ISLANDS

One book well worth borrowing from the library is called "Lost Island," by James Norman Hall. It is the story of some people living on a tiny pinpoint of an island in a group known as Polynesia. The story is fiction, but is termed "fiction of fact."

A man named George Dodd had been given a colonel's commission. He was sent to an atoll to transform it from a lovely little spot of beauty into a landing strip for American bombers. Living on the island were a father and daughter—the Lehmanns, Jewish refugees; Father Vincent, a Roman Catholic missionary; and a handful of natives. They were a happy, contented group.

Through the eyes of the author you can almost watch as this bit of green heaven set amidst a world of blue is invaded. The population is lifted bodily and transferred to another island to reestablish itself. Bulldozers strip the island of all its vegetation and cover the surface with asphalt.

Reading this story, you will probably feel dreadfully sorry for the people. You may feel they were badly mistreated, although their transfer was as gentle as possible. At first, this is all the story will mean to you. As you grow older though if you think about it very carefully you may begin to realize it really paints a picture of life.

Right now you are living at home with your family. You may have a nice home. Maybe you own a pet—a dog, a kitten, or some goldfish. Perhaps you have a room all your own. It is a familiar place. You are quite comfortable. You may remain here until you have finished high school. This is a lovely island where you are now. Once you leave, you can never return. It will be changed. You will be changed.

You decide to go away to college. The surroundings there and the friends you make will be wonderful too, but after a time you must leave college. This will become another lost island. The fun, the friends, and the hard work will become simply a memory.

Longing for a lost island can never do you good. Wishing to return will not accomplish anything. The law of life is that we move from one island to another. The past is a wonderful teacher. You can love the past, but you cannot live forever in the past.

LOST ISLANDS

When you are transferred to another island, get acquainted with it right away. Start enjoying it.

As each minute, each hour, each day, or each year goes by, you are moving further and further away from the days which are gone. What will tomorrow bring? We cannot tell. You are living today. Make the most of it.

THE NAME

Each tribe of American Indians has many interesting customs and legends. In one Western tribe, each brave was given several names. First was the one given him by his parents. This was usually determined by whatever the boy's father saw when emerging from the child's birthplace. A youngster might be called Full Moon, Bright Star, Twisted Twig, or any of a hundred names you could mention.

A boy's most important name was the one given him by the tribe to indicate what he was like, or what he had accomplished. He could be called Big Bear to indicate meanness, Swift Arrow to suggest how fast he could run, or Lazy Bones to show his indifference to work.

What about your name? Why did your parents give it to you? Was it the name of some favorite

THE NAME

relative or friend, or the same as your grandmother's or grandfather's? A little girl born in Massachusetts was called Gale because her father, a lobster fisherman, was out on the ocean in a storm when she came into the world.

Coca-Cola is the name given a drink by the manufacturer. The public christened it with another, shorter name: Coke. The manufacturers recognized the value of capitalizing on the public choice so they protected this second name by trade mark.

The names Nazarene or Christian sound very nice to us. However, in the early days of the Christian church these names were used to ridicule the followers of Jesus. According to the account in the book of Acts, the name "Christian" was first given to members of the church in Antioch. It was used as an expression of contempt. The early Christians could easily have refused the name. They could have ignored it, and after a time folks would have forgotten. To them, though, this was not a name of ridicule. It was a name worth sacrificing for and worth being sacrificed for. It was a name to be accepted and held dear.

To be a Christian means a lot. It means that a person is trying to be like Christ. It means that boys and girls know they should always be trying to do the right thing, to be different and better.

In the New Testament we read: "Let everyone who claims the name of Christian depart from wrongdoing."

BANQUETING ON A BOOK

Back in the 1930's, great windstorms carrying huge masses of dust swept across the prairies of some of our Midwestern states. Cattle died. Chickens died. There was no food. Everything was covered with drifts of dirt. Grasshoppers came. The grass was gone. They ate fence posts and barns and entered houses to eat the curtains at the windows and the clothing in the closets. People used up what little money they had had in savings accounts and had nothing left with which to buy food.

It's probably safe to say that even though at times you have said, "I'm starved," you've never really been hungry. Hopefully, you never will be. It is wise to remember, though, that there are many boys and girls living today who have never known what it means not to feel hungry.

The children of Israel wandering in the desert be-

BANQUETING ON A BOOK

came very hungry and cried out against Moses for bringing them into the wilderness. Moses was a very wise man. He saw lessons people could learn from being hungry. Moses recognized that God allowed the people to become hungry so they might be forced to change their attitudes and put their sights on something else. We read in our Bible: "And he humbled you and suffered you so that you should know that man does not live by bread alone."

A South Dakota man, who lived through the hunger after the dust storms, said that the words "Give us this day our daily bread" had little meaning for him until he, his family, and his friends were really hungry. He prayed. He read his Bible. There he found food for his soul. He became convinced that somehow things would work out. He remembered that as a child in Sunday school he had been told that John the Baptist had lived in the wilderness on grasshoppers and wild honey. He thought, "Why can't we do the same?" He gathered grasshoppers. His wife fried them. Soon his family began to regain strength. This man says that then he knew that God had answered his prayers for daily bread.

The Bible itself is food. But we humans find it hard to think of food save in terms of physical hunger. We assume the soul doesn't need food.

When Jesus was tempted by the devil to turn stones into bread, he said, "Man does not live by bread alone, but by every word that comes from the mouth of God."

IT TAKES
A LONG, LONG TIME

Fifty million years—how long is that? You don't know? Well, neither does anyone else. We can't even guess at that length of time because we have no means of comparison. We can understand what a year is. Some of us know the meaning of ten years as almost a lifetime. But fifty million is far too many years for us to grasp.

Geologists, men who study the crust of the earth, tell us that it took fifty million years to form the Grand Canyon. When you stand on the southern rim of the Canyon, you are about seven thousand feet above sea level. The plateau on which you stand, fifty miles long and thirty-five miles wide, is called "kaibab," which is an Indian word which means "mountain lying down."

IT TAKES A LONG, LONG TIME

There are many wonderful caves in the United States. Perhaps you have visited Mammoth Cave in Kentucky, Wind Cave in South Dakota, Luray Cavern in Virginia, or some other famous ones. One of the most beautiful is Carlsbad Caverns in New Mexico. At one time it was difficult and dangerous to visit and explore this cave, but today there is a good path leading into it and the trail is well lighted. There are guides, many of them college geology students, who can answer your questions.

In the caverns, way down in the earth, are some huge and breathtaking rooms. You may know that stalactites are those things like icicles which hang from the roof of a cave. They were formed as drops of water, working their way through limestone, feldspar, or some other kind of rock, carried with them minute specks of stone so small you couldn't see them even though you looked very carefully at the drop of water. When a drop of water became too heavy, it broke away from the roof, leaving behind it a bit of stone. Finally, these invisible mites, joining together, became visible stalactites. To form one took millions of years.

The beauty of the Grand Canyon and Carlsbad Caverns fills you with wonder, almost taking away your breath. If you stop to think how long it took God to form the cave and the Grand Canyon, you are even more awe-struck.

Many boys and girls want to do things in a hurry. One of the laws of life is that most things worth-

THE SQUIRREL'S BANK ACCOUNT

while take a long time. It takes a long time to learn to play the piano well. It also takes a long time to learn to paint a picture. It takes a long time to develop a good character.

Some very wise men wrote the books of our Bible. One of these men, in writing the ninetieth psalm, prayed: "So teach us to number our days that we may apply our hearts to wisdom."

WHAT ARE
YOU LOOKING AT?

The man who wrote the stories we have in the Acts was a medical doctor named Luke. Dr. Luke had had a lot of experience in recording cases. We can take for granted that what he tells us is as close to the fact as he could come.

He records that when Jesus left men for the last time, something happened which has never been understood. The disciples were gathered around Jesus. Then, it is said, "Jesus ascended." Somehow he just disappeared. But this disappearance was not the only strange thing that happened. The disciples thought they saw two unfamiliar men appear. It is written that one of these men spoke to the followers of Jesus, "Men of Galilee, why do you stand looking up into the sky?" If he had been speaking to you today he might have said something like, "Hey, you guys, what gives? Knock it off! Get with it!"

The disciples of Jesus had been with him for about three years and were well instructed as to what he expected them to do. But when he disappeared, they just stood looking up as if rooted to the ground. The stranger asked them a question that needed to be asked. They accepted the rebuke and went back to Jerusalem. We are told that Peter appeared before a lot of folks and more or less said to them, "Listen people, Jesus assigned jobs for us. He said we were to go into all the world talking about him and preaching love and understanding. And what are we doing? Nothing! Don't you think it's time we got to work?"

Often there are hard jobs to do, and rather than do them we'll figure out all kinds of excuses. Usually the excuses we give are "for the birds." They have no worth. What's more, we know it!

When Mother asks Fred why he is watching TV instead of doing his homework, Fred replies that he'll only stay another few minutes and then he'll start to study. What happens? Three hours later Fred is still in front of the boob tube and the homework is not done.

Boys and girls, like men and women, can think up lots of excuses for not doing the things they really should do. Or they sometimes can simply ignore the fact that work needs to be done.

THE HARVEST SEASON

After they first left Egypt, the children of Israel were a wandering people, but they soon began to settle down and cultivate the land. At that time, most farmers didn't live as the farmers in the United States do today—on their own individual farms. Rather, they lived in small villages from which they went out daily to their property in the surrounding countryside. This type of farm life is still practiced in some European countries.

Long before the children of Israel arrived in the Holy Land, the plains and terraced mountains had been cultivated. Probably men have been farming this area for nearly ten thousand years.

The prophet Hosea was a man of the country. He was concerned with wild and domestic animals. He knew the flowers and the fruits of the land. He talked about the weather, the sunshine, and the rain. Once he said, "They have sown the wind and they shall reap the whirlwind." Of course, he wasn't referring to wheat and rye, but to the behavior of the people We can learn many lessons from the harvest. One of the most important is, if you want good fruits and good grain, you must plant good seed, for what is reaped is dependent on what has been sown.

Harvesting, the act of gathering or collecting a ripened crop of grain, fruit, or vegetables, usually comes in the fall, which is a very beautiful season. The leaves of the trees turn shades of yellow, red, and brown before dropping gracefully to the ground. For some people this is a sad season. They think only of death, forgetting there is rebirth. It should be considered a happy time. The fallen leaves cover the roots of trees and tiny bulbs to keep them safe during the winter months. But that isn't all. They also become the food for the next spring's plants.

Life is like the seasons of the year—fall, winter, spring, summer, and then fall again. The preparation of the soil for the seed, the planting, the growing, the harvesting, make the complete circle. If you want a good life, if you want to be remembered, think good thoughts, do good deeds, live helpfully. The best fruit of all is a good name and the love of those who know you.

THOSE LITTLE THINGS

Lady Jane Grey was not only a beautiful girl but a brilliant one also. She spoke Greek and Latin and had some knowledge of Hebrew, Chaldee, and Arabic. All this in a day when most girls did not know how to read or write in their own language.

Jane's life was short and filled with sorrow. Her parents were harsh. Her home life was unpleasant. At an early age she became a ward of Thomas, Lord Seymour and went to live in his house. There she had riches but no happiness. A marriage was arranged between Jane and Lord Guildford Dudley. She entered into the marriage with the will to make it a success, but her husband never gave her a word of kindness or consideration.

Through intrigue, Jane and her husband were thrown into prison. If you visit the Tower of London, you may be able to see the room where Jane was kept. With a diamond, she scratched the tragedy of her life on a window pane—"my prison." A short while later, Jane and her husband were executed.

Jane had castles, land, titles, maids, all kinds of pretty clothing, but she never had what she craved the most—a kind word, a little bit of love, a sign of appreciation, a speck of understanding. She was beheaded at the age of sixteen.

We live in a world where the greatest gifts and sweetest blessings are often to be found in the little things. It was the lack of little things that killed Jane Grey long before the ax of the executioner. Jesus called attention to little deeds of faithfulness. He said, "If anyone gives so much as a cup of cold water to one of these little ones because he is a servant of mine, I tell you this: that man shall not go unrewarded."

When Jesus was in Bethany, a woman came up to him with an alabaster jar of very expensive ointment which she poured on his head. The disciples were indignant over the waste, but Jesus said, "She has done a beautiful thing." He also told of a widow who put in her last two bits of money in the church offering plate.

Sometimes it's the little things we don't do that are the most distressing. It's forgetting to make our beds. It's failing to smile or say "hello" when we pass people on the street. It's not remarking on someone's new clothing or new hairdo.

We've got to be careful of the little things.

BOXED IN

There is a very ancient Greek legend about Pandora, the first mortal woman. Zeus, god of the heavens, sent Pandora to earth as a punishment. He gave her a box filled with all human evils and ills but tucked hope at the bottom. When Pandora reached earth she opened the box, letting all the evils escape. But she closed the cover, leaving hope boxed in.

Did you ever own a Jack-in-the-box? There is a lot of difference between one of these and Pandora's box. A Jack-in-the-box is just for fun. It's a little clown on a spring. You push him down into the box so that the spring is all compressed and close the cover. When you loosen the lid, out he jumps. But, he can only come so far, for he's held in place by the spring. He can do no harm. He is designed to give pleasure.

THE SQUIRREL'S BANK ACCOUNT

In old England on May Day, there was sometimes practiced a custom called Jack-in-the-Green. A man or a boy would be placed in a box. Then the box would be covered over with green leaves. At a certain time during the May Day celebration, up "Jack" would jump, scattering the leaves. It suggested a flower opening and coming into full bloom and the new life expected with the coming of summer. The poet Alexander Pope wrote, "Hope springs eternal in the human breast." Given a chance, hope will always come forth.

Did you ever think of a boy or a girl as being in a box, or boxed in? Yes, this is very much the way all of us are. The **you** in us is all inside our bodies. What is that **you** like? Is it a pleasant thing that gives joy? Is it a **you** that gives kindness when it comes out of its box? Is it a **you** that is under control? Or is it a **you** that is mean, harsh, unkind, unlovely? Is it a **you** filled with wicked mischief which, when let out on the world, does only harm?

A psalmist once said, "Set a watch, O Lord, before my mouth. Keep the door of my lips." Perhaps he had been thinking about himself—of what he was like or what he could have been like.

CROSSING THE JORDAN

Since the very beginning of time, men have set up stones as memorials to various events in their experiences, to tell stories of their lives. The children of Israel made stone altars to remind themselves of their God. The Egyptians piled stones, one on top of another, until they created huge pyramids, believing the spirits of dead rulers would be housed in them. Early man carved the stones of the earth and made homes and temples in the stone walls of cliffs. The story of ancient America is shown in piles of stones left by Mayas, Aztecs, and Incas.

Recently, some stones were taken from the Jordan River which archaeologists believe had originally been placed there by the children of Israel to remind themselves of their crises, their failures, and their successes. Why had these stones been placed at this particular place? Because here the people had faced a crisis—they were about to cross the Jordan River.

All through your life you are going to come to new crossings of a Jordan—that is, new experiences which will demand effort. Life is not like sliding down a giant slide on a piece of burlap. It's more like climbing a mountain. This is true not only for individuals but for nations as well. The Colonies, the thirteen original states, had a Jordan to cross. People realized there could develop a permanent separation from England. Nearly all the prosperous and aristocratic men from Maine to Georgia were against the idea of revolution. The result was that Washington and his army almost perished at Valley Forge.

In his book "Abraham Lincoln: The Prairie Years," Carl Sandburg tells us that when Lincoln was presented to the nation as a candidate for president, of the several hundred ministers in Illinois there were not more than two or three on whom he could count for support. The ministers were afraid of the people in their congregations who said, "Can any good thing come out of the backwoods?" At this time, Abe Lincoln, all the ministers, and all the people of the congregations were standing on the bank of a Jordan, wondering if they should try to cross the rushing, dangerous waters.

Before long you will be going out on dates. Perhaps some of you are already dating. On those dates someone might say, "Let's do this." The "this" may be something you know your parents would not approve. You will be facing a Jordan. Should you or shouldn't you? The decision will not be easy.

Someday someone may say to you, "Let's take this." Whatever it is, it wouldn't belong to you. Taking it would be stealing. Yet you might think you could get by without being caught. You will be facing a Jordan. You will have to make a decision.

It is much easier to make decisions if you can talk over a problem with someone you can trust. God is always waiting to hear our problems, to help us cross a Jordan.

THE MARKS OF CHRIST

In 1968, news was flashed upon the world that a man who for years had borne the stigmata had just died. What is "stigmata"? The dictionary tells us that it is the plural of stigma. You know that stigma is a mark, a blemish, or a blot. So, stigmata must be marks, blemishes, or blots.

When Rome was in power, crucifixion was a common punishment for criminals. Usually they were bound to the cross with thongs, but special criminals were nailed to the wood. Jesus was judged worthy of being nailed. According to the New Testament, one of the guards standing beside the cross also wounded Jesus in the side with a spear.

When it is said that someone has borne the stigmata, it means that in some mysterious way, wounds have appeared on a person's hands, feet,

THE MARKS OF CHRIST

and side like the wounds on the body of Jesus. The first recorded example of this stigmatization seems to be St. Francis of Assisi. We are told that a woman named Louise Lateau started to have this strange affliction on April 24, 1868, and that every Friday her wounds would bleed.

This has happened again and again. People have tried to discover the reasons, but so far no one has offered an acceptable explanation.

Why then speak about the stigmata if no one knows what this means? Without doubt, Jesus was the greatest person who ever lived. He lived so wonderfully that ever since, men and women have been trying to be a little like him. Probably you will never see an example of the stigmata. There is even less possibility that you will ever carry these marks yourself, but you can be more like Jesus than you are. You can bear the marks of Christ more vividly and more tellingly than if you really had bleeding wounds. The marks of Christ that you carry in your heart will influence all you do or say and all of your relations with others. This is important.

SUBWAYS

Subways are among the great engineering accomplishments of man, constructed so folks can get from one place to another quickly. These underground railways often have been blasted through solid rock, or drilled through slime or sand.

Maybe you have ridden a subway in New York, Chicago, or Boston. Riding a subway can be fun. Life is very much like riding a train in a subway. You pick out a place to go and then find the train to take you there.

The train has to follow the tracks. Constantly the subway tracks need to be cleaned. Rubbish could litter the tracks. A very small object can cause a train to jump the tracks and hurl it against the side walls, injuring or killing many people. The driver of the train must obey the red and green signals.

SUBWAYS

All of us build subways. We call them habits. Some of our habits are extremely difficult to construct. They may take years to build. We need to know all about the subways we make, where they go, where they will take us. We need to know which train goes to which station, or we may get lost.

It seems incredible, but once a subway tunnel was lost. It happened near the South Station in Boston, Massachusetts. A whole section of the tunnel was unused for years, completely forgotten, lost.

The prophet Joel was a remarkable man who was able to see what might happen if people behaved in certain ways. He said, "They shall walk, everyone in his path."

The apostle Paul said, "Walk in the love of Christ."

THE UNDERTOW

Getting caught in an undertow is a strange, horrible, frightening, and sometimes fatal experience. An undertow is a current below the surface of the water which is moving in a different direction from the surface current. Oceanographers know and understand the many reasons for these undertows.

Often, in swimming areas, you may see signs reading: "Beware of the undertow." Just as people often pay no attention to signs saying, "Beware of the dog," they ignore the ones warning of undertow. They laugh and say, "What's an undertow to me?" Or, "I'm a good swimmer." But it makes no difference how good a swimmer you are if you are caught in an undertow; you might be carried out to sea before someone could rescue you.

An undertow is especially dangerous because you

THE UNDERTOW

can't see it on the surface. You stand and watch the waves as they break on the shore, seeming always to move toward the land. The surface looks so bright and safe you cannot realize danger lurks below.

One hot afternoon a man and some of his friends went swimming at a lovely beach just north of Tel Aviv. The Mediterranean was blue and beautiful. The water looked inviting. This man started to run out into the water. One friend shouted a caution. He had noticed that most people were sunbathing on the beach and that those who were in the water were where it was shallow. The friend said, "There might be an undertow!"

However, the man wasn't afraid. He'd been on the swimming team in college and was sure that no undertow could possibly bother him. He swam out into the sea. Suddenly, he felt as though giant hands were reaching up and holding his feet. No matter how hard he kicked he was helpless. The undertow twisted and turned his legs. Somehow he was able to get back to the shore.

Many times when a Mother or a Daddy says to a boy or girl, "Please don't go around with those kids," the young people question why. The parents cannot give a reason and say, "I don't know why but there's something." They might say, "Son, I'm afraid there might be an undertow. You can't see it but it's there and it may be dangerous." But like the man in Israel, the boy may not pay attention

THE SQUIRREL'S BANK ACCOUNT

to his parents' warning. Before he is aware he is caught. How? It may be heroin, LSD, cigarettes, or alcohol. It doesn't look dangerous. You are strong. You are different. You can do it and get by! Can you? Are you sure?

Right at the beginning of your Bible you have a story of temptation: "Now the serpent was more subtle than any beast of the field." There are many stories of temptation and the results that came. Watch out for the undertow.

THE SQUIRREL'S
BANK ACCOUNT

In arctic cold or desert heat, in far-off lands or in countries close to home, everywhere you go you can find squirrels. These little animals belong to the rodent family. They vary in size from that of a mouse—like a type found in West Africa—to the size of a cat—like the large black and white squirrels that live in Malay. The most common in North America are the gray squirrels who have the proper name of Sciurus carolinensis. There are also the familiar flying squirrels, red squirrels, black squirrels, and fox squirrels.

Squirrels are fascinating to watch. They are very playful and relatively tame. You can get quite close to one before he runs away. If you spend day after day giving him food to eat, he eventually gets to

THE SQUIRREL'S BANK ACCOUNT

trust you and will eat right out of your hand. You should be very cautious though, because squirrels can bite you and could infect you with the dreadful disease of rabies.

Have you ever seen a dog chase a squirrel? Squirrels will tease dogs, trying to provoke a chase. The squirrel is so fast he can dash up a tree almost in the wink of an eye. Then, he swishes his tail and chatters away at the dog below.

Mostly, squirrels eat nuts and fruits and vegetables, but they also like mice, small birds, and eggs. A squirrel will take a pine cone, and break away the leaves much as you break away the head of an artichoke. The difference is that you eat the tender leaves of the artichoke but the squirrel throws away the leaves of the pine cone and eats only the seed. The bits of cone which he discards go flying in every direction. He tears away the shell from the acorn and bolts down the nut which is inside in less time than it takes you to say, "Look at that squirrel!"

He doesn't bolt down all the nuts he gathers, though. The squirrel is foresighted. He lays in a supply of food for the winter. This is his "bank account." Each fall you can see him scurrying around picking up acorns, chestnuts, pine cones, all sorts of goodies for his winter use.

From the squirrel we can learn a valuable lesson: thrift. Many people today believe there is no need to be thrifty, to save for the rainy day or the winter months. They have developed the idea that if any-

THE SQUIRREL'S BANK ACCOUNT

thing happens to them, someone else will look after them.

In the Bible there are many references to thrift and waste. Perhaps you remember the story Jesus told about the young man who asked his father for his share of the inheritance that he would not have received until after his father's death. The father gave it to him and the young man went to a far country. We read: "The young man wasted his substance."

There is a lot of talk today about ecology. Man has discovered that his wastefulness has led to pollution. Something has to be done to correct the situation. We need to learn to be thrifty like the squirrels.